WHY PRAY?

No Prayer, No Power

A Prayer Guide for the Saints

Fay Ellis Butler, PH.D.

outskirtspress
DENVER, COLORADO

WHY PRAY? No Prayer, No Power
A Prayer Guide for the Saints
All Rights Reserved.
Copyright © 2014 Fay Ellis Butler, PH.D
v2.0

Outskirts Press, Inc.
http://www.outskirtspress.com

ISBN: 978-1-4787-3007-1

Library of Congress Control Number: 2014912070

Outskirts Press and the "OP" logo are trademarks belonging to Outskirts Press, Inc.

PRINTED IN THE UNITED STATES OF AMERICA

Dedicated to all

THE ENDTIME CHRISTIANS

Who have resolved to be the

very best that they can be for GOD.

TABLE OF CONTENTS

INTRODUCTION

"And ye shall seek me, and find me when ye shall search for me with ALL YOUR HEART" (Jeremiah 29:13).

Prayer is the language of the saints. The Word of God is the "road map" to heaven. Ignore both and eternal damnation is assured. **This book has been written to challenge the reader to become "kings and priests unto God" (according to Revelation 1:5, 6) by becoming men, women, boys, and girls full of faith and power through prayer and consecration.** This book details the diversity of prayer and the results of prayer in order to challenge us to be honest with ourselves and begin to deal with our powerlessness.

Note that there are many valuable institutions, groups, and auxiliaries in our church organizations which perpetuate the life of the organization. Many of us are hard-working church members who know how to make things happen. We have great preaching, great singing, great rejoicing, and great fellowship. However, we tend to operate in a "perceived" safety or comfort zone spending so much time with optional church activities[1] rather than with biblically mandated ones, like **prayer – petitions, intercession, supplications, seeking, praise and worship**.

Therefore, this book is based on the eternal and fundamental truth that the awesome power and presence of God becomes a reality in those who pray consistently; especially when he or she personalizes the Word of God in his or her prayers. **Satan does not fear <u>prayerless</u> anniversaries, <u>prayerless</u> Mothers' Boards, <u>prayerless</u> preaching, <u>prayerless</u> teaching, and <u>prayerless</u> churches.** In fact, Satan is laughing at us and accusing us night and day before God (Rev. 12:10), because we fail to pray as we ought. **He does tremble, however, at the humble, unknown or even weak saints on their knees praying in The Name of Jesus.** Why? Heaven is always stirred to war against the Devil on behalf of any member of the Blood washed Body of Christ, who prays.

Each individual must stand before God alone to answer the call placed upon his or her life. **There will be no excuses.** We cannot blame pastors, parents, or church leaders. It is true that the "apostle, prophet, evangelist, pastor, and teacher" are called to help perfect the saints (Ephesians 4:11-12). Whether those in the "fivefold ministries" do their jobs or not, it is still the individual's responsibility to seek God, to "draw nigh unto God", and to be faithful to Him.

> *"...Save yourselves from this untoward generation"*
> *(Acts 2:40).*

---

1   Rehearsals, Dinners, Fund Raisers, meetings, etc.

"...Work out your own salvation with fear and trembling" (Philippians 2:12).

If you have left 'your first love' and gone after things that do not profit putting positions of influence, money, and material things before pleasing God, simply STOP. You are made in God's own image and YOU have a will. You must choose to please God and to be pleasing in His sight.

". . .And him that cometh unto me I will in no wise cast out" (John 6:37). "I love them that love me; and those that seek me early shall find me" (Proverbs 8:17).

Each of us must stop and recognize the full importance of a life of prayer, and not just those words said on your knees at bedtime or that half hour in church. When you spend time EVERY DAY in the presence of God in prayer and in His Word, you will know the VOICE OF GOD. By knowing God's voice, you will not have, as so many have, **"the itching ear syndrome"** – always running to hear this prophet or that prophetess. **Would you go to a "palm reader"? Always looking for "a word" is the same as wanting your "palms read". (Not knowing the VOICE OF GOD is dangerous, considering the proliferation <u>of false prophets</u> in your church and my church, in your conventions and my conventions.)**

"For there shall arise false Christs, and false prophets, and shall show great signs and wonders; insomuch that, if it were possible, they shall deceive the very elect" (Matthew 24:24, see also I John 4:1).

Rather, you can consult God just as King David did – David always "inquired" of the Lord before going into battle.

> *"Let us therefore come **boldly unto the throne of grace**, that we may obtain mercy, and find grace to help in time of need"* (Hebrews 4:16).

God is waiting for each one of us to come and fervently seek Him so He can work with us and through us. The Body of Christ, collectively and individually, must be consumed with prayer.

Realize that almost all things from God are wrought through prayer.

- Why did you feel convicted enough to want to be saved?
  SOMEBODY PRAYED FOR YOU!
- What did it take for salvation?
  A PRAYER OF REPENTANCE and SURRENDER.
- What did it take to receive the Baptism of the Holy Ghost?
  A CLEAN LIFE and A HEART FULL OF PRAISE.
- What did it take to receive healing?
  THE PRAYER OF FAITH.
- What did it take to "cast the Devil out"?
  PRAYING IN THE NAME OF JESUS.

There is no quick fix but the solution is simple – BACK TO THE BIBLE. This book challenges you to develop a lifestyle and a prayer life that touches the Heart of God. Then make a powerful difference. Affect lives and churches for God!

PRAY until faith comes!

PRAY until the Fire of God falls!

PRAY until those cancers disappear!

PRAY until the saints' children take their rightful places in End-time Ministries!

PRAY until the "dead" churches become "houses of prayer for all people"!

"As it is the business of tailors to make clothes and cobblers to mend shoes, so it is the business of Christians to pray". Martin Luther (1834-1546).

PRAYER: WHAT IS IT?

Prayer is simply talking to and with God. However, in order to pray and get a hearing with God, God has to see His Son's Blood. In other words, you should be a child of God and an heir of God (Romans 8:17).

I. Do we really love God?

"And thou shalt love the Lord thy God with all thy heart, and with ALL thy soul and with ALL thy mind, and with ALL thy strength: this is the first commandment" (Mark 12:30; cf. Deut. 6:5).

Do you spend more time watching television, talking on the phone, going to business meetings and conventions, than in prayer and reading/studying the Word? Do you manage to spend more time on those things that give you personal pleasure like going to concerts, programs, watching television, shopping, ball games, etc., than seeking God?

*"If ye love me, keep my commandments. . .He that hath my commandments, and keepeth them, he it is that loveth me; and **he that loveth me shall be loved of my Father and I will love him and will manifest***

myself to him. . .If a man love me, he will keep my words; and my Father will love him, and we will come unto him and make our abode with him" (John 14:15, 21, 23).

First of all, if you want to be saved and effective in prayer, you must obey God. God's rules and commandments, first of all are instituted for man's protection and safety and secondly, so that He can bless those that obey Him.

Simple questions.

Do you obey those that God has given the spiritual oversight or leadership in your church?

Are you a THIEF in the sight of God? Do you PAY your tithes off all your increase? Tithes are the tenth of all your increase which belongs to God. **(You really haven't given anything when you PAY what you owe to God.)**

Do you share in offerings?

Do you distribute to the necessity of the saints (Gal. 6:10)?

Do you share with the needy (Matt. 25:34-40)?

Do you witness to unbelievers (Acts 1:8)?

Do you abstain from all appearance of evil (I Thess. 5:22)?

Do you watch and pray? (Luke 18:1)?

*"Whatsoever we ask, we receive of him, because we keep His commandments, **and do those things which are pleasing in his sight"** (I John 3:22).*

Secondly, once you willingly obey Him, He will manifest Himself to you because He knows you love Him. Make up in your mind to be as effective as possible in prayer. Prayer brings heaven down to the obedient child of God.

". . .For he that cometh to God must believeth that He is, and that He is a rewarder of them that DILIGENTLY SEEK HIM" (Hebrews 11:6).

Definitions Explored

Prayer is:

1. A reverent petition made to God

2. Any act of communion with God, such as **confession, thanksgiving, praise, worship, meditation, petition, seeking, supplication, intercession,** and **travail**.

There are numerous Greek nouns and verbs translating into English the one word *prayer*. For example, the Greek word "*enthuses*" is translated meaning "*prayer*" in some places, but very specifically "*intercession*" in other places. Or consider the verb "*akimbo*", meaning "*prayer*" in some places but may suggest "*wished for*" in other places. There are actually four different Greek verbs translating the word "*prayer*" and similarly just as many nouns for the word. This should suggest that prayer is highly diversified as to types of prayer and manner of praying.

TYPES OF PRAYER
CONFESSION
THANKSGIVING
PRAISE
WORSHIP
MEDITATION
PETITION
SEEKING
SUPPLICATION
INTERECESSION and TRAVAIL
FASTING and PRAYER

I. CONFESSION

Confession is simply admitting or acknowledging sins (Psalms 51:1) as well as assenting, declaring, and agreeing with God (Romans 10:9-10).

> *"That if thou shall confess with thy mouth the Lord Jesus, and shall believe in thine heart that God has raised Him from the dead, thou shall be saved. For with the heart man believeth unto righteousness, and with the mouth confession is made unto salvation" (Romans 10:9-10).*

Confession above all else has the quality of honesty and humility. Without these two elements, a prayer of confession is like "sounding brass and tinkling cymbal".

*"If we say we have no sin, we deceive ourselves, and the truth is not in us. If we **confess our sins**, he is faithful and just to forgive us of our sins, and to cleanse us from all unrighteousness" (I John 1:8-9).*

If individuals will not tell the truth and continue to sin, God will not hear or acknowledge their prayers.

"Now we know that God heareth not sinners: but if any man be a worshipper of God, and doeth his will, him will he heareth" (John 9:31)

Notice the tense *'heareth not'* suggests a continuation of not hearing. In other words, God will hear the sinner's prayer but there has to be some kind of change and commitment when praying to God. God knows all things about every individual.

"Neither is there any creature that is not manifest in His sight but all things are naked and opened unto the eyes of him with whom we have to do" (Hebrews 4:13).

Sincere confession helps the individual humble himself and makes room for God to be glorified in that person's life.

*"**I acknowledged my sin unto thee,** and mine iniquity have I not hid. I said I will confess my transgression unto the Lord; and thou forgavest the iniquity of my sin. For this shall every one that is godly pray unto thee in a time when thou mayest be found; surely in the floods of great waters they shall not come nigh unto him" (Psalms 32:5-6).*

II. THANKSGIVING

Thanksgiving defined is simply the giving of thanks for past and present events, that is, appreciating God for all He has done. Thanksgiving for all things acknowledges that God is in control even in what appears to be bad. It would sound absurd to begin praising God for cancer, multiple sclerosis, or anything incurable. But that fact of the matter is that Jesus bore all diseases on Calvary already has healed all diseases

> *"Who His own self bare our sins in his own body on the tree, that we, being dead to sins, should live unto righteousness; BY WHOSE STRIPES YE WERE HEALED" (I Peter 2:24).*

The healing that was already perfected on the Cross of Calvary is appropriated by thanksgiving and praise. Thanksgiving and praise produce and demonstrate faith. Furthermore, trials, tribulations and problems precipitate intense and persistent fasting and prayer which preface individual growth and spiritual POWER.

> *"In **EVERYTHING** give thanks for this is the will of God in Christ Jesus concerning you" (2 Thessalonians 5:18).*

Thanksgiving is gratitude.

> *"And let them **sacrifice the sacrifices of thanksgiving**, and declare his works with rejoicing" (Psalms 107:22).*

Where there is murmuring and complaining there is no thanksgiving. One must open his or her mouth and verbally tell God thanks (Psalms 51:15; 35:28)

*"Enter into his gates with thanksgiving, and into his courts with praise: **be thankful unto him and bless his name"** (Psalms 100:4).*

The "Gates of the Lord" are opened to you wherever you are. So when waking up in the morning, it's a new day, **thank God**. Even though "men ought to always pray" (meditate/talk to God, etc.), prayer should always include acknowledging God's love and protection **with thanksgiving and praise**.

Learn some of the Hebrew names for God and personalize them in your prayer. Remember in the first chapter of Genesis only "Elohim" (the plural of "El") was the name used for God and it means "The Mighty God". In the second chapter where man is first mentioned, we find the use of "Jehovah" which also means "The Mighty God" but additionally "The Mighty God Who reveals Himself to man. This term is entirely unique and personal for man. God demonstrates His infinite and limitless ways He deals with man. Therefore in the Hebrew you will find **Jehovah** hyphenated to demonstrate those specific needs of man being fulfilled by God. Since the Lord is the same yesterday, today, and forever, use these Names of God in prayer. This honors God, increases your faith and brings you into His Presence.

A. Jehovah-Jireh – "God, our Provider". *"God, thank you because you are my **JEHOVAH JIREH**, the Source of all things, and will supply all my needs, now and in the future".*

(Genesis 22:8-14).

B. Jehovah-Nissi – "God, our Conqueror" or "our Banner". *"God, I thank you because you are my JEHOVAH-NISSI and will go before me and fight my battles".* (Exodus 17:15).

C. Jehovah-Rapha – "God, our Healer". *"God, I thank you because you are my JEHOVAH RAPHA, the healer of my home, emotions, and body".* (Exodus 15:26).

D. Jehovah-m'Kaddesh – "The Lord who Sanctifies". *"I thank you because even though Satan brings up past feelings, thoughts, and desires. I cleanse myself daily in Your Blood. I am clean because you are my JEHOVAH-m'KADDESH, my sanctifier".* (Exodus 31:13; Leviticus 20:8).

E. Jehovah-Tsidkenu – "God, our Righteousness". *"I thank you because you are my JEHOVAH-TSIDKENU; my righteousness is of you and I am IN YOU and you are in me".* (Jeremiah 23:6; 33:16). *"For He hath made Him [Jesus] to be sin for us [on the Cross of Calvary], who knew no sin; that we might be made the righteousness of God in Him"* (2 Corinthians 5:21).

F. Jehovah-Shalom – "God, our Peace". *"In times of danger, destitution and death, I still can have peace because you are my JEHOVAH-SHALOM, my Peace-giver".* (Judges 6:23, 24).

G. Jehovah-Rohi – "God, our Shepherd". *"God, I shall not want for anything, you are my JEHOVAH-ROHI, my eternal Care giver".* (Psalms 23:1).

H. El Shaddai – "The All Sufficient One or the Almighty God". *"I gladly yield and submit to you, you are my EL SHADDAI, you are more than enough for every need that I have"*. Genesis 17:1.2.

I. Adonai – "The Majestic Lord who is worthy of Worship". *"Gladly, I submit to the Lordship of Jesus because as ADONAI you are my Master (LORD)"*. Psalm16:2

III. PRAISE

Praise and worship is glorifying God for who He is. Even though we generally interchange praise and worship, praise is something anyone can do, as the psalmist wrote, *"Let everything that hath breath, praise ye the Lord" (Psalms 150:6)*. WORSHIP HAS EVERYTHING TO DO WITH HONORING GOD FOR WHOM HE IS: NOT JUST FOR WHAT HE HAS DONE.

"Ah Lord God! Behold, thou hast made the heaven and the earth by thy great power and stretched out arm, and THERE IS NOTHING TO HARD FOR THEE: Thou shewest loving-kindness unto thousands, and recompensest the iniquity of the fathers into the bosom of their children after them; the Great, the Mighty God, the Lord of hosts, is His name; Great in counsel, and mighty in work; for thine eyes are open upon all the ways of the sons of men; to give every one according to his ways, and according to the fruit of his doings. . ." (Jeremiah 32:17-19).

Praise is defined as the means to extol, to laud, to honor, to acclaim.

Praise may take numerous forms:

YOUR BODY

1.   **Standing:**
     *"Praise ye the Lord. Praise ye the Name of the Lord; praise him, O ye servants of the Lord. Ye that **STAND** in the house of the Lord, in the courts of the House of our God"* *(Psalms 135:1-2).*

2.   **Kneeling:**
     *"O come, let us worship and **bow down**: let us **KNEEL** before the Lord our maker (Psalms 95:6).*

3.   **Dancing:**
     *"Let Israel rejoice in him that made him: let the children of Zion be joyful in their King. Let them praise him in the **DANCE**: let them sing praises unto him with the timbrel and harp" (Psalms 149:2-3).*

4.   **Leaping:**
     "Blessed are ye, when men shall hate you, and when they shall separate you from their company, and shall reproach you, and cast out your name as evil, for the Son of man's

*sake. Rejoice ye in that day, and **LEAP FOR JOY** for, behold, your reward is great in heaven: for in the like manner did their fathers unto the prophets" (Luke 6:22-23).*

YOUR VOICE

1. **Mouth:**
   *"I will GREATLY PRAISE the LORD with my **MOUTH**; yea I will praise him among the multitude" (Psalms 109:30).*

2. **Singing:**
   *"Speaking to yourselves in psalms and hymns and spiritual songs, **SINGING** and making melody in your heart to the Lord" (Ephesians 5:19).*

3. **Shouting:**
   *"So David and all the house of Israel brought up the ark of the Lord with **SHOUTING** and with the sound of trumpet" (II Samuel 6:15).*
   See also Isaiah 12:6.

YOUR HANDS

1. **Lifting your hands:**
   *"I will therefore that men pray everywhere, **LIFTING UP HOLY HANDS,** without wrath and doubting" (I Timothy 2:8).* See also Psalms 134:2.

2. **Clapping:**
   "O CLAP YOUR HANDS, all ye people;
   shout unto God with the voice of triumph"
   (Psalms 47:1).

3. **Instruments:**
   "Moreover David and the captains of the host
   separated to the service of the sons of Asaph,
   and of Heman and of Jeduthun, who should
   *prophesy with **HARPS**, with **PSALTERIES**,*
   *and with **CYMBALS**. . ." (I Chronicles 25:1).*
   See also Psalms 150:3-5.

The manner of praise may be determined by your personality and your church tradition, but PRAISE GOD because:

1. Praise is strength.

*"And Nehemiah. . .said unto the people, this day is holy unto the Lord your God; mourn not, nor weep. For all the people wept, when they heard the words of the Law. Then he said unto them, Go your way. . .for this day is holy unto our Lord: neither be ye sorry; for the **joy of the Lord is your strength**" (Nehemiah 8:9-10).*

"Therefore with JOY shall ye draw water out of the well of salvation" (Isaiah 12:3).

2. Praise represents faith

*"**Wherein ye greatly rejoice,** though now for a season, if need be, ye are in heaviness through manifold temptations: **That the trial of your faith,** being much more precious than of gold that perishes, though it be tried with fire, might be found unto praise and honor and glory at the appearing of Jesus Christ" (I Peter 1:6-7). See also Isaiah 61:3.*

3. Praise brings deliverance

*"And when he had consulted with the people, he appointed singers into the Lord, and that should praise the beauty of holiness, as they went out before the arm, and to say, Praise the Lord: for his mercy endureth forever. **And when they began to sing and to praise, the Lord set ambushments against the children of Ammon, Moab and Mount Seir, which were come against Judah; and they were smitten"** (2 Chronicles 20:21-22).*

IV. WORSHIP

Praise is worship and worship is praise. The main difference is that **while everyone can praise the Lord, only the saints can worship Him because He enters their praises** (Psalms 22:3).

Most times the people of God miss out on the Glory of God's presence because they rarely go from thanksgiving to worship. Further, individuals may wait to be stirred to praise through choir singing or someone else praying. <u>Worship for the child of God is not a choice, it is a loving duty!</u> Further, **praise and worship are never based on your feelings.**

What are the purposes of worship?

1. To fellowship with God and minister to the Heart of God.

> *"But thou art holy, O thou that inhabitest the praises of Israel."(Psalms 22:3).*

2. To place yourself close to God.

> *"Draw nigh unto God, and he will draw nigh unto you. . ." (James 4:8)*

3. To acknowledge the awesome power of God and your trust in God and to demonstrate your love without reservation. **Your adoration and worship of God have nothing to do with the circumstances (good or bad) of your life.**

> *"For we are the circumcision, which worship God in the spirit, and rejoice in Christ Jesus, **and have no confidence <u>in the flesh</u>**" (Philippians 3:3).*

Worship and Adoration is the way the people of God minister to God in love. The worship experience must **FOCUS ONLY ON GOD.** Personal experience is eliminated entirely. Of course you appreciate salvation, healing, and deliverance. However, worshiping God is the verbal, mental, and spiritual recognition of the awesomeness of God. Tell

God and mean it:

"I LOVE YOU LORD"

"I EXALT YOU LORD"

"I PRAISE YOU FOR YOUR MAJESTY AND DOMINION"

"YOU ARE THE EVERYWHERE GOD WORKING YOUR WILL"

"YOU ARE THE ARCHITECT OF THE UNIVERSE AND

THE CREATOR OF THE ENDS OF THE EARTH"

"I MAGNIFY YOU"

"HOW EXCELLENT AND GREAT IS THY NAME"

"I AM GLAD TO WORSHIP YOU, IF I HAD A THOUSAND TONGUES TO PRAISE YOU, IT STILL WOULD NOT BE ENOUGH"

"I CHOOSE TO GLORIFY YOU"

Use some of God's Hebrew names while worshiping Him.

1. Yahweh/Jehovah – "The God who always is and never changes".

2. Jehovah-Olam – "God the Everlasting One".

3. Jehovah-Elyon – "The Lord God Most High".

How do we worship?

1. In spirit and in truth with your voices, hands, trumpets, drums, etc. (2 Chronicles 5:11-13; Ezra 3:10-13).

"But the hour cometh, and now is, when the true worshipers shall worship the Father in spirit and in truth: For the Father SEEKETH such to worship him. God is a Spirit: and they that worship him must worship him in spirit and in truth" (John 4:23-24).

There can be no verbal ritualistic platitudes in worshiping God. Since God is a Spirit and is everywhere, in order to fellowship with Him (even though we use our mouths), we must worship Him with our innermost being (our spirit) which has been filled with the Holy Spirit. Jesus, the Spirit of Truth, has given us the Holy Spirit which allows us to worship in Spirit and in Truth. **In the same way that Abel's sacrifice was his best and was accepted, so too must we worship God with our best without reservation.** You know that God is pleased with the worship experience when He presents Himself with the Glory of His Presence. **What are the deep things embedded in your/our worship?** HUMILITY, REPENTANCE, and TOTAL SURRENDER. (2 Chronicles 6:11-21).

What are the results of real/total worship?

The services with total worship are the services in which God is pleased to come in and demonstrate **HIS GLORY WITH MIRACLES** (2 Chronicles 5:11-14; 7:1-3). How sad it is when the Glory of God comes in while the saints are worshiping, and the flow of God's Glory is cut off because someone starts an emotional display like dancing. Every time the Spirit of God moves throughout the congregation is not automatically a time for praising the Lord in the dance. Dancing is in order when praising God for personal victory, such as Moses' sister Miriam did when she danced after they crossed over into Canaan (Exodus 15:20-21) or when David danced when the Ark came back to Israel (II Samuel 6:12-14). The "worship experience" is centered on God and is about God.

V. MEDITATION

Meditation is continual reflection on God and His Word. Luke 18:1 reads "we ought to always pray and not to faint". Praying **is not only verbalization of thoughts, problems, praises, and/or feelings to God,** but it is also **thinking, pondering, and honoring the things of God.** Meditation therefore is a mindset, an attitude, and a lifestyle.

> *"This book of the law shall not depart out of thy mouth: but thou shalt **meditate therein day and night**, that thou mayest observe to do according to all that is written therein: for then thou shalt make thy way prosperous and have good success" (Joshua 1:8).*

"But his delight is in the law of the Lord; and in his law doth he meditate both day and night" (Psalms 1:2).

There are so many of life's distractions and problems that we voluntarily lend our minds and thought processes to hours of unprofitable television watching (for perceived relaxation). As children, before the age of television, DVDs, videos, high tech computer gadgets, and games, CD's, the worldwide web, etc., we knew that the *"heavens declared the glory of God"* (Psalms 19:1). We did not know the names that man gave the clouds, like cirrus, nimbus, stratus, cumulus, but we could look up at the clouds and pick out shapes of animals, cars, birds, or whatever. We may not have been meditating, but we were certainly focusing on God's grandeur. Oftimes we would catch fire flies and wonder; catch beautiful butterflies and wonder; find a four-leaf clover in the grass and wonder. Unfortunately today with an overabundance of hitech easily available entertainment, too many Christians are not even aware that their faith is being weakened because of diminished devotions and sincere praise.

*"I remember days of old; I meditate on all thy work;
I muse on the work of thy hands" (Psalms 143:5).*

In 1996, I was on a missionary trip to Guyana, a tropical, humid, water logged country. I saw the largest tree that I had ever seen in my life. It would have taken at least four men with arms stretched to encircle the tree. The thing that was so intriguing was the leaves. The leaves were so dense; it had to be billions on that one tree. Thinking about the awesomeness of God, I said to God, "just like you have numbered every hair on every head, you know the exact number of leaves on that tree".

Some simple things may seem inconsequential but if you ponder or meditate on the source -- God, surely faith will increase. The volcano, the earthquake, the tsunami (tidal wave) are all controlled by God, just like the ant colony and the bee hive. Meditating on the Word of God as well as on the mighty handiworks of God, increase faith

> *"Let the words of my mouth, and **the meditation of my heart**, be acceptable in thy sight, O Lord, my strength and my redeemer (Psalms 19:14).*

VI. PETITION

> *"**Ask and it shall be given you;** seek and ye shall find, knock and it shall be opened unto you" (Matthew 7:7).*

Petition is defined in the dictionary as a solemn request to a superior authority. **Petition** in the Bible suggests personal requests as in Philippians 4:6, *"Be careful for nothing; but in everything by prayer and supplication with thanksgiving, **let your requests be made known unto God"**.*

1. A **petition** can be an isolated request.

   a) As in Elisha's prayer for spiritual vision for his servant who feared the surrounding enemy (2 Kings 6:17).

b) As in Solomon's prayer for wisdom (I Kings 3:5-9).

c) As in Jabez's prayer for prosperity in his work (I Chronicles 4:9).

2. **Petitions** will definitely be part of your regular prayers. Your **petitions** can be the times you consult God about any and every thing that affects your personal life. **Recall how often David inquired of the Lord for direction** (I Samuel 23:2; 30:8; 2 Samuel 2:1; 5:19, etc.) Therefore, during your prayer time or any time during the day, you can **PETITION THE LORD**. For example, when you get up in the morning, "Lord, what will you have me to do for the ministry today"?

> Or if you must do school shopping for five children with $100, ask the Lord to lead you to the store with the best sales.

> Or, if you are traveling and lost, pray simply, "Lord, show me the right direction".

> Or, when you misplace your keys or eyeglasses in your own home, just ask the Lord to help you find them.

What concerns you, concerns God. We actually dishonor God's love by ignoring Him. Consulting Him by requesting guidance and/or help is like a child's relationship to his or her father.

Prerequisites for petitions to be answered.

1. You must have a life in God (John 15:16). See I Samuel 28:6.

2. There must be faithful (Matthew 17:20).

3. The **petitions** must not violate the Will of God (I John 5:14-15).

VII. SEEKING

To seek means to search for, to look for, and to inquire after.

"One thing have I desired of the Lord, <u>that will I seek after;</u> that I may dwell in the house of the Lord all the days of my life, to behold the beauty of the Lord, to inquire in his temple" (Psalms 27:4).

Seeking the Lord infers process, continuity and subsequently growth.

*"Sing unto him, sing psalms unto him, talk ye of all his wondrous works. Glory ye in his Holy Name: Let the hearts of them rejoice that **SEEK THE LORD**. . .Seek the Lord and his strength, **seek his face continually**" (I Chronicles 16:9-11).*

It involves the soul of man – will, intellect, emotions. Too often a lot of words and moaning, based on church traditions, are considered seeking. **Seeking**, however, is really the sum total of "striving after", "requesting", and "coveting earnestly".

> *"For I know the thoughts that I think toward you, saith the Lord, thoughts of peace, and not of evil, to give you an expected end. Then shall ye call upon me and ye shall go and pray unto me, and I will hearken unto you. And ye **shall seek me**, and find me when **ye shall search for me with all your heart**" (Jeremiah 29:11-13).*

Therefore "the seeking mode" means that your heart,[2] your hunger and longing are turned toward the things of God. **"Seeking the Lord" has some preconditions attached to it – specifically doing the things that are right and quit doing those things you know are wrong.** Repent and "do your first works over again". God cannot respond to seeking where there is unrighteous living.

> *"Sow to yourselves in righteousness, reap in mercy, break up your fallow ground: for it is time to **SEEK THE LORD** till he come and rain righteousness upon you" (Hosea 10:12).*

> *"But **seek ye first** the kingdom of God, and all his righteousness; and these things shall be added unto you" (Matthew 6:33).*

1. **Seeking the Lord** and His righteousness means that you do not have to seek Him for material things. Delight yourself

---

2   The heart of man represents the center of the will and desires.

in seeking Him, serving Him, obeying Him, and He will give you the desires of your heart (Psalms 37:4).

2. **Seeking the Lord** means that you take nothing for granted, knowing that the Lord may not be available to you on your terms. (Compare Genesis 6:3 with 2 Corinthians 13:5).

*"**Seek ye the Lord** while he may be found, call ye upon him while he is near..." (Isaiah 55:6).*

3. In your **seeking, pray the promises of God** that are applicable to your needs and you will definitely be praying the will of God.

"And this is the confidence that we have in him that if we ask ANYTHING according to his will, HE HEARETH US; and if we know that he hear us, whatsoever we ask, we know that we have the petitions that we desired of him" (I John 5:14-15).

VIII. SUPPLICATION

*"Praying with all prayer and **supplication** in the spirit, and watching thereunto with all perseverance and **supplication** for all saints" (Ephesians 6:18).*

Supplication is passionate prayer filler with humility and hunger while seeking special favors or blessings. In the Old Testament, putting on "sackcloth and ashes" demonstrated supplication with desperate humility which usually included fasting.

*As the hart panteth after the water brook, **so panteth my soul after thee, O God**. **My soul thirsteth
for God**, for the living God; When shall I come and
appear before God? My tears have been my meat day
and night, while they continually say unto me, where
is thy God? When I remember these things, I pour out
my soul in me; for I had gone with the multitude, I
went with them to the house of God, with the voice of
joy and praise. . ." (Psalms 42:1-3).*

*"Lord all my desire is before thee; **and my groaning**
is not hid from thee" (Psalms 38:9).*

*"Whom have I in heaven but thee? And there is none
upon earth **that I desire beside thee**" (Psalms 73:25).*

In other words, to be most effective in supplicating God,
include all that is mentioned. Yell, cry, groan, and roll on
the floor, if you want. But know that above all, that you are
desperately, fervently, and passionately supplicating God. It
does not matter if the church is full or empty, or who is next
to you. It concerns you and your desperate hunger for God.

1. In **supplication**, there is confession and petition.

Daniel had been taken to Babylon during the reign of
Nebuchadnezzar, served under Belshazzar and was still in
Babylon when Darius, the Mede reigned. He read the Words
of the prophet, Jeremiah and felt the great urgency to pray
desperately for the condition of those in captivity. (See
Daniel 9)

"And I set my face unto the Lord God, to seek by prayer and supplications, with fasting and sackcloth and ashes: And I prayed unto the Lord my God, and made my confession, and said, O Lord, the great and dreadful God, keeping the covenant and mercy to them that love him, and to them that keep his commandments; We have sinned and have committed iniquity, and have done wickedly, and have rebelled, even by departing from thy judgments...O Lord, according to thy righteousness, I beseech thee, let thine anger and thy fury be turned away from thy holy city Jerusalem" (Daniel 9:3-5, 16).

2. In **supplication**, there is no doubt.

"And now, O God of Israel, let thy word, I pray thee, be verified, which thou has spakest unto thy servant David my father. But will God indeed dwell on earth? Behold, the heaven and heaven of heavens cannot contain thee; how much less this house that I have builded? YET HAVE THOU RESPECT UNTO THE PRAYER OF THY SERVANT and to his supplication, O Lord my God, to hearken unto the cry and the prayer, which thy servant prayeth before thee today" (I Kings 8:26-29).

3. There is no debate in your spirit concerning your desire for God.

4. There is total communion and surrender in the spirit of man (John 4:24).

IX. INTERCESSION AND TRAVAIL

Even though the basic definition of prayer is "seeking God", **intercession is specifically "seeking" for another person or some situation.**

> *"I exhort therefore, that first of all, supplications, prayers, **intercessions**, and giving of thanks be made for all men" (I Timothy 2:1).*

Intercession is *"effectual fervent"* or *"prevailing prayer"*. It is effectual because it will have the desired effect sought for. In other words, it will touch the heart of God. To **pray prayers of intercession** effectively, the object of your prayers must have a great measure of importance to you and to God. Further, your **intercession** must be for the right motive.

Definitions

Intercession(s) derive from the Greek word "enteuxis" which denotes a lighting upon, then, a conversation. In other words, it means getting a hearing on behalf of another, then presenting petitions. **To make intercession** from "entunchano" means literally "to meet with and plead with a person for or against others".

From Webster's dictionary, **intercession** means "entreaty in favor of another". "Inter", the prefix, means both "mutually" and "together". "Cession" means "the act of surrendering". **Intercession, therefore, is the act of putting one's personal needs and desires aside, and praying for another**

or a situation with continued intensity until the answer is given, the problem solved or the burden lifted. (Review Moses' prayers for Israel in Deuteronomy 9:7-26).

"Ye have been rebellious against the Lord from the day that I knew you. Thus I fell down before the Lord forty days and forty nights, as I fell down at the first; because the Lord had said he would destroy you. I prayed therefore unto the Lord, and said, O Lord God, destroy not thy people and thine inheritance, which thou hast redeemed through thy greatness, which thou hast brought forth out of Egypt with a mighty hand. Remember thy servants, Abraham, Isaac, and Jacob; look not unto the stubbornness of this people, nor to their wickedness, nor to their sin. . ." (Deuteronomy 9:24-27).

1. **Intercession** always has a sense of importunity. To importune means to beg, urge, insist, and demand relentlessly. The word derives from Medieval Latin, "importundri" meaning to be troublesome.

2. **Intercession** includes the qualities of insistence and persistence.

3. At the same time, there must be absolute faith and also the feeling of absolute inadequacy.

4. **Intercession** is never general or random; it is never just "saying prayers".

In **Intercession, God is glorified.** The child of God sets aside his or her needs, agenda, desires, tiredness, even hunger and prays to God on behalf of others. **Intercession** takes at least two forms:

1. The individual feels a burden for something and goes to God with consistent intensity or,

2. God places "**a spirit of intercession**" in the believer. This is the time when God Himself has control of the believer's prayers and the Holy Ghost uses the believer to intercede.

Every believer who has surrendered to God on God's terms automatically becomes an intercessor. There will be times when God, night or day, will bring a need or a person before you with a burden that will not go away. It is time to pray.

EXAMPLE

A minister who I may see once or twice a year came before me with such heaviness. I began praying. I called the minister only to find out that the "enemy, Satan, had come on like a flood" and everything that could go wrong was going wrong. The situation was so critical, the minister had decided to give up his ministry and quit working for God. The Holy Ghost had quickened my spirit to pray before I knew the problem. When the problem was understood, the Holy Ghost stirred me not to only intercede but to war against Satan's "conspiracy of evil". The "stronghold of the enemy was torn down" and demolished.

The Requirements of Intercessory Prayer.

1. You cannot truly **intercede** if you are not totally surrendered to God.

*"If ye **abide in me**, and my words abide in you, **ye shall ask what ye will**, and it shall be done unto you" (John 15:7)*

2. There must be evidence of absolute humility, coming in the presence of God. See Daniel's prayer in Daniel 9 and Jesus' **intercessory prayer** in John 17.

3. **You must pray IN THE NAME OF JESUS.** This means that you stand before the throne in the character and power of Jesus.

4. You must pray in the Will of God (I John 5:14-15).

*"And this the **confidence** that we have in Him, if we ask **any thing** according to His will, He heareth us. And if we know that he hear us, whatsoever we ask, we know that we have the petitions that we desired of him".*

5. There must be perseverance in prayer:

*". . .The effectual **fervent prayer** of a righteous man availeth much" (James 5:16).*

POWERFUL prayers from you on earth can command **POWER FROM HEAVEN.** No one can limit the power of God in you but you. **PRAYERLESSNESS IS POWERLESSNESS.**

*"I have set watchmen upon thy walls, O Jerusalem which shall never hold their peace day or night: ye make mention of the Lord, **keep not silence,** . . .**and give Him no rest"** (Isaiah 62:6-7).*

The Model of Intercession

Review Luke 11:5-8.

1. You must recognize an urgent need: *"the hungry friend at midnight".*

2. There must be willing love: *"He sacrificed a night's rest for the hungry friend".*

3. There was a sense of impotence. The man went begging for his friend because he had nothing to give him.

4. The friend had faith that he could somehow meet the need.

5. Importunity prevailed. In spite of apparent refusal of a neighbor, the friend persisted and finally received bread. **For prayers to be answered, we must see and feel the necessity for holding on anyhow. This means that in intercession there is perseverance, determination, and intensity – REFUSAL TO ACCEPT DENIAL.** (Remember Jacob wrestling all night with the angel until he blessed him. See Genesis 32:24-32).

6. There must be confidence of reward (Deuteronomy 4:29).

There are many types of prayer, all of which may take place during your prayer hour. You may however worship and praise the Lord for one hour and never ask for anything. On the other hand, we should never petition or seek the Lord without first praising and honoring him. Never forget, God is the architect of the universe and the giver of life. Everything, we need He has! However, NEVER, NEVER TAKE GOD FOR GRANTED. Commune with Him, Praise Him, petition Him, meditate on the mystery of His Love and mercy, and intercede for others.

Prayer is the language of the saints. People who are skilled in their professions or vocations are competent and proficient enough to communicate the language of that discipline. If you know God at all, knowing Him in Spirit and in Truth qualifies the believer to become proficient in prayer. Remember, it is not the multiplicity of the words, but sincerity, persistence, and consistency that counts.

FASTING and PRAYER

Fasting is simply going without food, nourishment, and sometimes water. **Fasting and prayer, like intercession, is seeking God at a fuller level of intensity**. Further, there are levels of anointing and power that the individual will never achieve without a commitment to consistent fasting, praying, and studying the Word of God. There are no "short cuts" to power.

Why Fast and Pray?

1. In desperate times of great need (Ezra 8:21-23).

> *"Then I proclaimed a fast there, at the river Ahava, that we might afflict ourselves before our God, **to seek of him a right way for us, and for our little ones**, and for all our substance. For I was ashamed to require of the king a band of soldiers and horsemen to help us against the enemy in the way; because we had spoken unto the king, saying, The hand of our God is upon all them for good that seek him but his power and his wrath is against all them that forsake him. So we fasted and besought our God for this: and he was entreated of us."*

2. To know the reality of God's Shekinah Glory in you and your church (Isaiah 58).

"Is this not the fast that I have chosen? To LOOSE the bands of wickedness, to UNDO the heavy burdens, and to let the oppressed go free, and that ye BREAK EVERY yoke? . . .Then shall thy light break forth as the morning, and thine health shall spring forth speedily: and thy righteousness shall go before thee; the glory of the Lord shall be thy reward. . .And they that be of thee shall build the old waste places: thou shalt raise the foundations of many generations; and thou shalt be called, the repairer of the breach, the restorer of paths to dwell in" (Isaiah 58:6, 8,12).

3. To humble oneself (Psalms 35:13).

"But as for me, when they were sick, my clothing was sackcloth: I humbled my soul with fasting. . ." (Psalms 35:13).

4. To be able to cast out powerful demons (Matthew 17:14-21).

*"And Jesus rebuked the devil: and he departed out of him; and the child was cured that very hour. Then came the disciples to Jesus apart, and said, why could we not cast him out?. . .Howbeit this kind goeth not out but **by prayer and fasting**" (Matthew 17:18, 19,21).*

5. In times of danger (Esther 4:16; 2 Chronicles 20:1-27;

Acts 27:9).

> *"It came to pass after this also, that the children of Moab, and the children of Ammon, and with them others beside the Ammonites, came against Jehoshaphat to battle. . .And Jehoshaphat feared, and set himself to seek the Lord, and proclaimed a fast throughout all Judah. . .And all Judah stood before the Lord, with their little ones, their wives and their children. . .And he said, Hearken ye, all Judah and ye inhabitants of Jerusalem, and thou King Jehoshaphat, Thus saith the Lord unto you, Be not afraid nor dismayed by reason of this great multitude; for the battle is not your's, but God's. Ye shall not need to fight in this battle; set yourselves, stand ye still, and see the salvation of the Lord with you, O Judah and Jerusalem. . ." (2 Chronicles 20:1, 3, 13, 15, 17).*

6. <u>For public calamities</u> (2 Samuel 1:12).

> *"And they mourned, and wept, and fasted until even, for Saul, and for Jonathan his son and for the people of the Lord, and for the house of Israel; because they were fallen by the sword" (2 Samuel 1:12).*

7. <u>When reading the scriptures</u> (Jeremiah 36:6).

> *"Therefore go thou, and read in the roll, which thou hast written from my mouth, the words of the Lord in the ears of the people in the Lord's house upon the fasting day. . ." (Jeremiah 36:6).*

How to fast?

"Moreover, when ye fast, be not as the hypocrites, of a sad countenance; for they disfigure their faces, that they may appear unto men to fast. Verily I say unto you, they have their reward. But thou, when thou fastest, anoint thine head and wash thy face; that thou appear not unto men to fast, but unto thy Father which is in secret: and thy Father, which seeth in secret shall reward thee openly" (Matthew 6:16-18).

Types of Fasts

1. The Supernatural Fast.

The **supernatural fast** is a divinely called **fast**. However long the "fast", the person will go through successfully without damage to the body because it is a "fast" that God ordained and called. Notice that usually a person can fast without anything for a few days. In any event, even in a total fast, after three days, some fluids should be taken.

Examples of **supernatural fasts**.

A. Forty Day Fasts

- **Moses, fasting** 40 days and nights without food or drink, received the tables of stone written by the finger of God. Notice this **fast** was so powerful while he was in the presence of God, his face shone with the Glory of God and had to be covered.

- **Elijah**, one of the great prophets of the Bible, ran and hid from Jezebel after the great contest with the prophets of Ball. He fasted without meat in the great mountain of God. Mount Horeb (part of Mount Sinai) for forty days and nights. After this supernatural fast, he was free of all fear (I Kings 19).
- **Jesus**, prior to beginning his ministry, was tempted in the wilderness as he fasted 40 days and nights without drink or food (Matthew 4:1-11; Luke 4:1-13).

B. Twenty-one Day Fasts

- Daniel took it upon himself to fast for twenty-one days because he was "SEEKING AN ANSWER" to the strange vision God had given him (Daniel 10:3-10).

C. Fourteen Day Fasts

- In Acts 27, Paul went through a 14 day fast for DELIVERANCE when he was being taken to Rome as a prisoner to be tried before Caesar.

D. The Solemn Assembly

- When destruction of every magnitude is "at the door" of your home, church and/ or community, **a solemn assembly** is in order (Joel 1:14; 2:12-16). **A solemn assembly is a consecration of the entire church**.

2. Regular Fasts

- These are the fasts which help bring and keep you into a right relationship with God through self-discipline as well as help you to become more effective in the work that God has assigned to your hands (2 Corinthians 6:4-5). These fasts help "crucify the flesh".

*"But in all things approving ourselves as the ministers of God, in much patience, in afflictions, in necessities, in distresses, in stripes, in imprisonments, in tumults, in labors, in watchings, in **fastings**. . ." (2 Corinthians 6:3-5).*

A. **One day fast or 24 hour fast.** Most Pentecostal churches ask their members to fast at least two days per week. Fasting was a normal part of worship in the New Testament churches. See Acts 13:1-2; 14:23.

B. **Three day fast**, particularly in times of desperation.

- Esther and her people were about to be wiped off the face of the earth by Haman; She called a three day fast (Esther 4:13-16).
- Jehoshaphat and the Israelites were surrounded and about to be destroyed. Jehoshaphat fasted and sought God for an answer and deliverance (2 Chronicles 20).
- God was about to destroy Nineveh. The King of Nineveh pleaded to God for mercy and had everyone including babies and every animal had to fast. God spared the city at that time (Jonah 3, 4).

"And God saw their works, that they turned from their evil way; and God repented of the evil, that he had said that he would do unto them; and he did it not" (Jonah 3:10).

C. Seven day fast.

3. Methods of Fasting

A. **The Fast without food or drink.** These fasts, unless God specifically demands otherwise, should not last longer than three days. If more days are called for, individuals should begin drinking water.[3]

B. **Fasting without food but drinking water.** Water is not a food and has no nutrients. The body is 80% water and you may lose 2 to 5 quarts from evaporation (breathing and perspiring). Water helps the body's temperature to remain constant.

C. **The "no pleasant bread" Fast** (Daniel 1). This is the fast that no meats, sweets, or favorite beverages are taken. Notice the word "pleasant" from the Hebrew word "chamadoth" really refers to delicacies. Some people claim that this was a "lentil only" fast.

D. **The non-total Fast.** This is the fast during which

---

3   Recognize that when your body begins rebelling with headaches and dizziness, etc., your body is getting rid of toxins from perhaps too many refined carbohydrates like cake and meats (which more are more difficult to digest than fruits and vegetables) and which may also be full of hormones and chemical tenderizers. Withdrawal (during the fast) from caffeinated beverages like tea, coffee, Pepsi, and cola drinks may result in headaches also.

individuals take a little form of nourishment in the form of juices, which contain a few calories and some minerals. This will help to prevent nausea and griping. Notice that the juice should be diluted and not refrigerator cold. These juices should be taken a few sips at a time, not gallons.

Fasting for the Wrong and the Right Reasons

1. The Wrong Reasons

A. To appear to gain recognition and honor (Matthew 6:16-18).

B. Out of pride and arrogance (Luke 18:12-14).

C. For strife (Isaiah 58:4-5).

D. Fasting only when you want God's help (Jeremiah 14:11; Zechariah 7:5).

E. Fasting without repentance strengthens the devil in the person that is fasting. **This is a sure way to become "bound".** For example, if an individual with some unresolved spiritual issues (like unforgiveness) goes on a consecration (fasting and prayer) with the church or decide to go on a consecration alone, there may be some serious spiritual consequences. If this individual has unforgiveness, bitterness, and/or anger towards anyone, which they have not dealt with or refused to deal with, a "doorway" is opened to the spirit-man. Satan will strengthen that unforgiving spirit, because "after all", that person will think, "I am trying. I am fasting". The spirit of man cannot be "sealed" and protected by the Holy Spirit until all uncleanness is bound and cast out. This happens when a person repents and totally surrenders every area of their life at "the new birth" or it happens during the personal sanctification process. Every unclean spirit that is ignored becomes stronger in the person especially during a consecration which equals **bondage**.

On the other hand, if an individual recognizes the problem of bitterness, anger, lust, or whatever, and goes to God in prayer with all humility and honesty and consecrates to conquer the problem and to be totally delivered, that is different. This is the means of preventing or conquering bondage.

2. The Right Reasons

A. To humble one's soul (Psalms 35:13; compare Psalms 109:24).

B. To draw oneself from the carnal state into a spiritual state, where God can talk to the believer and the believer can hear God; and to stimulate spiritual faculties.

C. To strengthen and increase the faith of the believers in a local congregation as well as strengthen the prayer ministry.

D. To assist individuals in crucifying the flesh (putting to death evil in the mind and emotions); e.g., lust, fornication, adultery, homosexuality, lesbianism, backbiting, bad habits (smoking, drinking, drugs, gossiping) stealing (including not paying tithes correctly). Some individuals may have to fast constantly to resist and defeat demonic assault from powerful old abominable desires and habits.

E. To give necessary power to cast out demons (Matthew 17:14-21).

The greatest thing about God's love and God's glory is that no man can limit any man. God responds and gives to each Christian according to how much he/she demonstrates the "hunger" for God. We demonstrate spiritual hunger with **FASTING, PRAYING,** and **STUDYING THE WORD OF GOD.**

PRAYER: WHY PRAY?

"Call unto me and I will answer thee, and shew great and mighty things which thou knowest not" (Jeremiah 33:3).

Why pray?

1. Pray because **God loves you very much and wants to be in a relationship with you**. (Remember He did sacrifice His Son to make provision for our atonement). You are important to God but will never know it until you start seeking and praying to God. Jesus said, *". . .Him that cometh to me, I will in no wise cast out" (John 6:37)*. Individuals can pray for you but the only means of having a relationship with God is **first of all**, <u>through your own prayers</u>. You are the only one that can repent for you; it is <u>through prayer</u>. The great things that count in heaven and for eternity are wrought <u>through prayer</u> – salvation, deliverance, healings, revivals, etc. Further, the only way ministry in anyone's life is going to be developed by God, is **first of all** is <u>through prayer</u>.

2. **Jesus told us to pray**, and in fact taught prayer (Matthew 6:3). Further, God is so powerful, so awesome, and so omniscient, we dare not take Him for granted and assume God

is going to work for us anyhow. Every person, even the new born babe is just a breath or a heartbeat away from death. God and His Word are the only things that will live forever. If the Word is "tabernacled in us", because we prayed and continue to obey and pray, we too have everlasting life.

> *"The voice said Cry. And he said What shall I cry?*
> *All flesh is grass. . .**Surely the people is grass. The**
> ***grass withereth, the flower fadeth: but the Word of***
> ***our God shall stand for ever"** (Isaiah 40:6-8).*

> *"Heaven and earth shall pass away **but my words***
> ***shall not pass away"** (Matthew 24:35).*

3. **Prayer builds faith**. Pray until the Spirit of God anoints your praying, and then the Holy Ghost will pray through you as well as give you what to pray about.

> *"But ye beloved, building up YOURSELVES on your*
> *most holy faith, **praying in the Holy Ghost"** (Jude*
> *20).*

This does not necessarily mean praying in a heavenly language, but rather that you pray so fervently that you know the Holy Spirit is directing your prayers.

Whatever you need – <u>revival, healing, or your children saved, PRAY AT THE LEVEL OF GOD'S MIGHT, and not at the level of your need</u>. God knows your needs but you cannot take God for granted. Even though biblical reality and miracles may seem distant to you, **none of God's power or Everlasting Greatness has diminished**. It simply is that our prayer time has decreased with a corresponding increase in unbelief. Study the Word, increase your prayer time and watch faith increase. To build your faith, every time you pray thank God for His Majesty and mighty works. **Thank Him for being the same yesterday, today, right now, and forever**.

Deal with the matter of God's awesome power working one day or two days ago challenges our faith in God as our **"Ever-present Help in the Time of Trouble"**.

Try different strategies to begin building your faith. Find the approximate date of occurrence of some of your favorite miracles from a Bible handbook or a good study Bible. Write them down. After the dates of your favorite miracles are written, then estimate how many days ago the miracle occurred in God's timing. **Time is only a construct God created for man**. Recognize that **a day is as a thousand years with God**. (God's day could also be as long as 10,000 years because God is from everlasting to everlasting).

The year 2000 AD is equal to a mere two days in God's timing. Estimate the days of God's timing by adding the years before Christ (BC) and the years after Christ (AD). Calculate how many days ago the event occurred if 1000 years are equal to one day. For example, God opened the Red Sea for Moses and the Red Sea in approximately 1500 B.C. We are now in 2000 A.D. (which equals 3500 years ago). **That means that just three and one half days ago in God's time**, God changed his own gravitational laws and opened the Red Sea for His people. Therefore don't hesitate to include God's miracles and changelessness in your prayers: **"God, you are**

MY MIGHTY GOD, who changes not, who opened the Red Sea just 3 ½ days ago. God, I need help, healing, deliverance, etc."

Find a minimum of 10 miracles in the Bible. For example:

- The birth of Isaac to Sarah at 91 years old and Abraham at 100 years old was in approximately 1900 B.C. (Genesis 21:5). **1900 B.C. + 2000 A.D. = Almost 4000 years ago or 4 days ago in God's timing.**
- All the plagues against Egypt while the children of Israel in Goshen were "plague-free" in approximately 1300 B.C. (Exodus 9:26; 10:22-23, etc.). **1300 B.C. + 2000 A.D. = Almost 3500 years or 3 ½ days ago.**
- Or "the opening of the Red Sea" for the children of Israel where they walked across on dry ground. Approximately 1300 B.C. **1300 B.C. + 2000 A.D. = Almost 3500 years or 3 ½ years ago.**
- Elijah called down fire from heaven in the contest with the prophets of Baal. (I Kings 18:24-38). Or, the aged Elijah ran faster than Ahab drove his horse drawn chariot back to his palace. Approximately 850 B.C. (I Kings 18:49). **850 B.C. + 2000 A.D. = A little less than 3000 years or almost 3 days ago.**
- The lost axe head swam for Elisha. 825 B.C. (II Kings 6:6). **825 B.C. + 2000 A.D. = Less than 3000 years or almost 3 days ago.**
- The bones of Elisha resurrected a dead man when the dead man's body touched Elisha's bones in 800 B.C. (II Kings 13:20-21). **800 B.C. + 2000 A.D. = 2800**

years or approximately 2 ¾ days ago.

- The ambush God caused against the Ammonites, Moabites, and the Edomites when King Jehoshaphat sent Judah first with singing and praises. Approximately 850 B.C. (II Chronicles 20:1-30). **850 B.C. + 2000 A.D. = 2850 years or almost 3 days ago**.
- The thousands of demons cast out the demoniac called Legion by Jesus. 32 A.D. (Mark 5:9-15). **At the beginning of the first A.D. millennium, 32 A.D., over 2000 years ago = 2 days ago**.
- Or the feeding of more than five thousand from five loaves and two fishes. Approximately 32 A.D. (Matthew 14:19-21). **Over 2000 years ago or 2 days ago**.
- Or the 3000 saved in one day when the Holy Ghost fell. 33 A.D. (Acts 2:41). **As above, 2 days ago**.
- Or the shadow of Peter healing people. 33 A.D. (Acts 5:15-16). **As above, 2 days ago**.

4. God has an innumerable host of angels that He will dispatch when your life pleases Him and/or when you really pray.

*"Are they not **all ministering spirits**, sent forth to minister for them who shall be heirs of salvation?" (Hebrews 1:14).*

For example, the people of God were praying for Peter, who was in jail and about to be killed and the Angel of the Lord led him out of the prison (Acts 12:7). God sent an angel to shut up the lions' mouths when Daniel was thrown in the lions' den (Daniel 6:22). God even sent another angel who was bringing a message to Daniel because HE PRAYED (Daniel 10:10-14).

How have we missed out on the many blessings and healings from God because we have become too busy to pray? One young man said that he had a vision of heaven and that God had a huge warehouse full of new eyes, ears, knees, even teeth, but He is unable to send them to the saints because there is little prayer and less faith coming up to Him. When you are faithful to the call of God – winning souls, serving the saints, praying, and consecrating – God will send whatever number of angels He needs to send to keep you protected and doing what you do for God.

<u>Example</u>

Evangelist John Gordon of Chicago, Illinois, is a mighty man of God and a servant of the Body of Christ. He will assist and do whatever it takes to get the job done for God, whether street, prison, or mission field ministry or even building church edifices.

He testifies how he had come home from church very late one night, parked his car and was turning to enter his home. Two men, armed, approached him to rob him. Suddenly, they looked frightened and ran. He turned around and saw two angelic beings, massively and perfectly formed, dressed in long army type trench coats. They stood until he went into his home. When he had called his

wife to come and look, they were gone.

5. Pray because it is normal and natural for God, the architect of the universe and the creator of the Earth, to do the unnatural, WHEN THE PEOPLE OF GOD PRAY.

*"And another angel came and stood at the altar, having a golden censer; and there was given unto him much incense, that he should offer it with the **PRAYERS OF ALL SAINTS** upon the golden altar which was before the throne. And the smoke of the incense, which came with the prayers of saints, ascended up before God out of the angel's hand. And the angel took the censer, and filled it with fire of the altar, and cast it into the earth; and there were voices, and **thunderings and lightnings and an earthquake**" (Revelations 8:3-5).*

For example. . .

Paul and Silas, in spite of their severe whipping, sang and prayed at midnight. The Scripture does not say they prayed for an earthquake or even for their freedom. It said simply, **". . .they sang and prayed at midnight. . ."** and God sent AN EARTHQUAKE which shook the foundations of the prison and the doors opened, hence their freedom (Acts 16:25-26).

When the Philistines were coming against the children of Israel, they fasted cried, and prayed. However, Samuel, the last judge of Israel, cried unto the Lord for Israel and offered a young lamb to the Lord as a burnt (sin) offering, ". . .***THE LORD THUNDERED*** *with a great THUNDER on that day* *upon the Philistines, and discomforted them; and they were smitten before Israel"* (I Samuel 7:3-10).

Example

In the early thirties, Charles Harrison Mason, founding father of the Church of God in Christ was in a summer Convocation in the old Temple on South Wellington Street in Memphis. There were no air conditioners, no fans and no insulation. It was sweltering heat, without a breeze. The saints were hot; some fainting from heat exhaustion. Dad Mason, as he was called by the saints, stopped the service long enough to REBUKE the heat IN THE NAME OF JESUS. Immediately, a cool breeze began to blow in the building just like air conditioning. The saints were revived and had church.

Example

In the late twenties, one of the sisters of the church came across the Mississippi River from Arkansas to Memphis to see S.T. Samuels, Bishop Mason's right hand man. S.T. Samuels was a man of great faith for miracles. He fasted everyday until 6:00 P.M. and prayed constantly. It was late spring. The woman complained that because of the drought, there were no vegetables (like salad greens) coming up and the people were tired of beans. Further, not only the spring crops were dying in the fields but so were the summer seedlings. S.T. Samuels put his

fist up and REBUKED the drought IN THE NAME OF JESUS. They saw a black cloud rise up out of the Mississippi River and moved over that area in Arkansas. A torrential rain came down which normally would have destroyed the struggling crop. However, the woman came back in TWO DAYS and testified that not only had the spring crop come up but summer crops like cucumbers and tomatoes were ready for picking.[4]

There are many awesome ministries that God has ordained for the Body of Christ. However, because there are more "programs" and "meetings" to make people feel good, than to encourage people to pray without ceasing, God's Glory does not appear in most of our services. God is all too often not really "the center of attraction". Notice the proliferation of "prosperity ministries", the "praise specialists", "prophets", "prophetesses", "bishops", "retreats", and "conferences". **But where are the ordinary brothers and sisters who can pray for the sick, or cast the devil out and liberate he oppressed and possessed?**

Through prayer **In the Name of Jesus**, every saved individual has access to God. Jesus told us, *"If ye abide in me, and my words abide in you, ye shall ask what you will, and it shall be done unto you" (John 15:7). "For through* Him (Jesus), *we both have access by one Spirit to the Father" (Ephesians 2:18).*

---

4   This is personal communication from my father, Elder Ralph N. Ellis, Sr., now deceased who went to Bishop C.H. Mason's church (in Memphis, Tennessee) in 1922 and was a member until he migrated to New York in 1937.

6. The only way to have power over all that Satan sends is through fasting and prayer. Singing, dancing, rallies, programs, professional erudite preaching, attending retreats and conventions may help church growth and fellowship but <u>do not give POWER.</u> Jesus specifically stated that some types of demonic attack and possession *". . .goeth **not out** BUT BY FASTING AND PRAYER"* (Matthew 17:21).

Satan is "prince of this world", "prince of the powers of the air", "prince of devils", and the "prince of darkness". He is loosed for a little while longer and he does have power, but only over those who are not IN CHRIST. He is <u>not</u> King and he is <u>not</u> Lord. Therefore, your ability to remain IN CHRIST to have POWER over all the power of the enemy, Satan, depends on your absolute surrender to the LORDSHIP OF JESUS and your prayer life. Jesus said,

> *"Behold, I give unto you **POWER** to tread on serpents and scorpions and **over all the power of the enemy**, and NOTHING shall by any means hurt you"* *(Luke 10:19).*

- Satan can hinder but he cannot stop you.

> *"Wherefore we would have come unto you, even I Paul, once and again; but Satan hindered us"* *(I Thessalonians 2:18)*

- He can send trials and afflictions but they won't remain.

> *"The righteous cry, and the Lord heareth, and*

*delivereth them out of all their troubles. . .Many are
the afflictions of the righteous; but the Lord delivereth him out of them all" (Psalms 34:17,19).*

- Satan can send torment and fear, but he is only successful if you accept torment and fear (II Timothy
  1:7)

*"Fear thou not; for I am with thee: be not dismayed;
for I am thy God; I will strengthen thee; yea, I will
help thee; yea, I will uphold thee with the right hand
of my righteousness" (Isaiah 41:10).*

Over and over again we are commanded to:

"Pray without ceasing. . ." (I Thessalonians 5:17)

**"Praying always with all prayer and supplication. . ."
(Ephesians 6:18)**

"Continuing instant in prayer. . ." (Romans 12:12)

**"In everything by prayer, let your request be made known
unto God" (Philippians 4:6)**

"Watch ye therefore and pray always. . ." (Luke 21:36)

"Men should pray everywhere. . ." (I Timothy 2:8)

"Continue in prayer. . ." (Colossians 4:2)

"Men ought always to pray, and not to faint" (Luke 18:1)

"Seek the Lord and His strength, seek His face continually" (I Chronicles 16:11)

Remember, prayer brings heaven down and releases miracles that God has stored up for His people. Remember you are as powerful as your prayer life. Wigglesworth Smith, a mighty evangelist in England during the early part of the twentieth century, coined the succinct but true phrase:

MUCH PRAYER – MUCH POWER

LITTLE prayer – LITTLE power

NO prayer – NO power

PREREQUISITES
OF PRAYER

If Jesus had to teach his disciples to pray, we obviously also need to be taught and to be disciplined in prayer. Satan is pleased when we are limited to "cheering squad prayers", "emptying spiritless humming", "vain repetitions", and "prayer-time-nap-taking".

I. Praying as JESUS taught us to PRAY.

Step one

From Matthew 6:9, the Lord's Prayer starts out with *"Our Father which art in heaven, hallowed be thy name."* The word "hallowed" comes from the same root word as "hallelujah" which means "praise the Lord", or more specifically, "boast in the Lord".

Boast in the Lord because He is your healer, peace giver, deliverer, way maker and you can talk to Him at any time. We ought to begin all our prayers with praise and worship because praise ministers to God. He will commune with the saints by entering their praises with an anointing (Psalms 22:3; See

Psalms 100:3). Praise and worship is the atmosphere where God is pleased to bring heaven down and work miracles.

Step two

"Thy kingdom come, thy will be done in earth as it is in heaven." This is in fact a higher dimension of praise because you are praying "let King's Dominion come in me and in the Earth just like in heaven. What are all the hosts of heaven doing? Praising God and obeying absolutely. Essentially worship is the humbling of ourselves so much that we forget our needs, problems, and situations and worship God in complete submission and obedience to His will as the heavenly hosts, that is, the angels. Be specific as you pray 'Thy Will be done". Pray *"Thy Will be done in Me, in my family, in my home"*, *"Thy Will be done in my church and my community"*, etc.

Step three

"Give us this day our daily bread." Only after we completely submit to God do we bother petitioning God for our own personal necessities, as well as for the needs of others. Notice the "our" in "our daily bread". Remember, you do not have to seek God for fringe benefits. They come subsequent to first seeking the kingdom of heaven and all its righteousness (Matthew 6:33) and delighting yourself in working for God (Psalms 37:4).

Step four

"Forgive us our debts" more accurately, refers to our sins; in other words, forgive us for our sins. We are not perfect even as we strive toward perfection. Therefore, lest we have sinned and offended the heart of God with sins, deeds, idle words, thoughts and/or actions, we must repent every day.

Step five

"As we forgive our debtors" or those who hurt us, sinned against or who have done us wrong. We must continually forgive because God loves everyone including the vilest sinner. He forgives everyone who repents including the vilest sinner. No one is greater than God. When we don't forgive, then the Father, who changes not, cannot forgive us (Matthew 6:14-15).

Remember, if we are truly saved, Satan, the prince of this world, will send offenses (Matthew 18:7) because he wants the saints to fail. Your protection against failing God is twofold. **First, always remember, God loves everyone equally; and second, that no person should have so much power over you that you fail God with the "demon of unforgiveness".**

Step six

"Lead us not into temptation, but deliver us from evil." God obviously does not lead anyone into temptation. Our prayer in this phrase is "Lord as we allow you to lead us, give us the discerning that we need and help us to know the enemy of our soul. Strengthen me so I won't be overpowered by Satan".

Step seven

"For thine is the kingdom, the power, and the glory, forever, Amen." We must end our prayers with praise and worship. Praise tells the Lord that you are satisfied and happy because you have committed everything into his hands. Praise is faith and increases faith.

Can I *"PRAY"* The Lord's Prayer?

I cannot say *"OUR"* if I live in a watertight spiritual compartment; if I think a special place in heaven is reserved for my denomination.

I cannot say *"FATHER"* if I do not demonstrate the relationship in my daily life.

I cannot say *"WHICH ART IN HEAVEN"* if I am so occupied with earth that I am laying up no treasure over there.

I cannot say *"HALLOWED BE THY NAME"* if I, who am called by His Name, am not holy.

I cannot say *"THY WILL BE DONE"* if I am questioning, resentful, or disobedient to His Will for me.

I cannot say *"IN EARTH AS IT IS IN HEAVEN"* if I am not prepared to devote my life here to His service.

I cannot say *"GIVE US THIS DAY OUR DAILY BREAD"* if I am living on past experiences.

I cannot say *"FORGIVE US OUR DEBTS AS WE FORGIVE OUR DEBTORS"* if I harbor a grudge against anyone.

I cannot say *"LEAD US NOT INTO TEMPTATION"* if I deliberately place myself or remain in a position where I am likely to be tempted.

I cannot say *"DELIVER US FROM EVIL"* if I am not prepared to fight in the spiritual realm with the **WEAPON OF PRAYER**.

I cannot say *"THINE IS THE KINGDOM"* if I do not give the King the disciplined obedience of a loyal subject.

I cannot say *"THINE IS THE POWER"* if I fear what men may do or what my neighbors may think.

I cannot say *"THINE IS THE GLORY"* if I am seeking glory for myself.

I cannot say *"FOREVER"* if my horizons are bounded by the things of time.

I cannot say *"AMEN"* if I do not also add, COST WHAT IT MAY, for to pray this prayer it honesty will cost **everything**.

---Anonymous---

II. How to reverently approach "THE THRONE OF GRACE"

1. Prayer is properly addressed to the Father (Matthew 6:6,9; 16:23).

   *"Ye have not chosen me, but I have chosen you, and ordained you, that ye should go and bring forth fruit, that your fruit should remain: that whatsoever ye shall **ASK OF THE FATHER** in my name, He may give it you"(John 15:16).*

2. Prayer is also properly addressed to Jesus. *"And whatsoever ye shall ask in my name, that will I do, that the Father may be glorified in the Son. If ye shall ask anything in My name, I will do it" (John 14:13, 14).* See also Acts 7:59.

In no instance in the New Testament, do you read of anyone praying to the Holy Ghost or in the Name of the Holy Ghost. The Holy Ghost testifies of Jesus (John 15:26), because the Holy Ghost is the Executive Agent of the Godhead bringing about the Will of the Father and the Son in the Earth. The Holy Ghost resides in the believer (John 14:16-17) to teach him and to help him pray in the Name of Jesus (John 14:26). Praying in THE NAME OF JESUS was so important, that Jesus ordered it at least six times.[5]

---

5   John 14:13-14; John 15:16; John 16:23-24,26.

3. Your prayers, as a saint of God, offered IN THE NAME OF JESUS (John 14:13), must be in accord with His Character, what He stands for and His Will. In other words, your life should be totally surrendered to God, confident of what He is able to do and will do. Praying in THE NAME OF JESUS is **authority** – "carte blanche" to power. *"If ye shall ask anything in my name, I will do it" (John 14:14).*

4. Pray until YOU FEEL IT! See Luke 22:40-44.

III. Pray with humility

*For thus saith the HIGH and LOFTY that inhabiteth eternity, whose name is Holy, **I dwell** in the high and holy place, **with Him also that is of a contrite and humble spirit**, to revive the heart of the contrite ones" (Isaiah 57:15).*

Humility is born by looking at God, His Holiness, His Majesty, and His Power, and then looking at man's human frailty – without power or might. Once the awesomeness of God is comprehended, then gladly one should be able to praise Him and seek Him. Therefore, to be clothed in humility is also to be clothed in prayer.

<u>Definitions</u>

Humility is the quality of being humble, possessing modesty and the lack of pride. In the Bible, **humility** means "lowliness of mind, "humbleness of mind". See Romans 12:3.

"Be of the same mind one toward another, Mind not high things, but condescend to men of low estate, Be not wise in your own conceits" (Romans 12:6).

Compare Philippians 2:5-9. See also I Corinthians 3:18-21.

The Old Testament use of the word "humble" renders differences in meaning; "to be submissive, modest and lowly" as in Micah 6:8 ("hiphil"), or "to let oneself be trampled upon" as in Proverbs 6:3 (Hithpael). In the New Testament, the word "humble" means "to abase oneself, bring oneself low" as in James 4:6 and I Peter 5:5.

Since the innate nature, the sin nature, in each of us tends toward gratifying oneself; we must constantly work on humbling ourselves. Willfulness, selfishness, self-pity, stubbornness, disobedience, "showing off" are all part of the sin nature which we must constantly "put to death" or mortify (Colossians 3:5). "Putting to death" or mortifying the sin-nature is an operation of the individual's will and has to include some regular times of consecration.

1. We must not only pray fervently and sincerely, but we must humble our souls with fasting (Psalms 35:13). Eating good food is a pleasurable comfortable activity. Denying oneself food, hence pleasure, lets God know you are willing to deny yourself to draw closer to Him.

2. Essentially when we come to God in consecration, or any time we need to recognize ourselves as nothing in relationship to God's awesome POWER and MAJESTY (Review Job 38).

3. We need to recognize our insufficiency (2 Corinthians 3:5), knowing that death is always one breath away. We must acknowledge that it is God that provides the means for us to be sustained. We know that disaster and hard times may be an "earthquake away", "a tornado away", or "a hurricane away".

4. We must always bear in mind that we must work on ourselves, because we do not want to have "a **Nebuchadnezzar Experience**" (Daniel 4:30-34), because of pride.

5. On the other hand, we need to be thrilled and awed by His matchless marvelous mercy, as well as His desire for fellowship with us; His willingness to work for us (Jeremiah 33:3). Review James 4:6, 10; I Peter 5:6. Compare Proverbs 16:5, 18-19.

"Come unto me ALL ye that labor and are heavy laden, and I will give you rest. Take my yoke upon you and learn of me; for I am meek and lowly in heart: and ye shall fine rest unto your souls. For MY YOKE IS EASY and MY BURDEN IS LIGHT"(Matthew 11"28-30).

"Behold, I stand at the door and knock; if any man hear my voice, and the door, I will come in to Him, and will sup with him, and he with me" (Revelation 3:20).

IV. Prayers are unanswered because:

1. Self-righteousness (Luke 18:1-8).

2. Vain repetitions and "entertaining" prayers (Matthew 6:5, 7).

3. Refusal to humble oneself and refusal to stop overt and covert wickedness (II Chronicles 7:14-15).

4. Selfishness and refusal to help the poor (Proverbs 21:23).

5. "Spots" are not washed from the heart (Psalms 66:18).

6. The "spirit of unforgiveness" (Psalms 66:18).

7. Petitioning for the wrong reason (James 4:3).

8. Refusal to accept or hear the Word (Proverbs 28:9).

HOW TO PRAY THE WORD OF GOD

"Finally my brethren, be strong in the Lord. . .that ye may be able to stand against the wiles of the devil. . .Wherefore take unto you the whole armor of God. . .the sword of the Spirit, which is THE WORD OF GOD; praying always with all prayer and supplication in the Spirit. . ." (Ephesians 6:10-11, 13, 17-18).

Have you stopped to consider the deep things of the Word and how powerful praying the Word is?

1. In the beginning was **The Word (Jesus)** and with **The Word (Jesus)** spoke everything into existence (except of course, man whom He formed with His hands).[6]

*"For by **HIM** [Jesus] were all things created, that are in heaven, and that are in earth, . . .all things were created by Him, and for Him: and He is before all things and by Him all things consist" (Colossians 1:16-17).*

---

6   See Genesis 1:3,6,9,11,14,20,24. Everything was spoken into existence.

2. You, the saint of God, **are born of incorruptible Seed (Jesus), by the Word of God (Jesus), which abideth and liveth forever** (I Peter 1:23). Therefore, you are IN CHRIST (2 Corinthians 5:17).

3. **Jesus is THE WORD.** In the beginning was **THE WORD** (John 1:1). Then **The Word** was made flesh and *"dwelt among us"* ("tabernacled in us" as the literal translation goes) (John 1:14). Because we are born of **THE WORD** and we are in **THE WORD** (in Christ), we have all the rights of SONSHIP (Romans 8:17).

4. **Now consider the awesome effectiveness of the saint praying THE WRITTEN WORD (appropriate Bible verses), to THE WORD, Jesus, who is "tabernacled in us" (John 1:14), who is our advocate (I John 3:1) sitting on the right hand of the Father making intercession for us (Hebrews 7:25).**

Praying simple prayers without a lot of embellishments IN THE NAME OF JESUS is always powerful because Jesus Himself told us to pray in His Name (John 14:14; John 15:7). The Father responds because He recognizes us as sons and daughters because of the Blood of Jesus applied to our lives. However, consider the awesomeness of the saint praying **THE WRITTEN WORD to THE WORD, JESUS,** who is **"tabernacled in us".** Similar to intensifying prayers from petition to travail and intercession, we move the level of our praying from praying in the Name of Jesus to praying the Written Word in the Name of Jesus. Obviously, Jesus knows His own Word, since He is the Word and The Word is Everlasting Truth. **There is no need to beg God.**

Thank Him for His Word as you agree with the truth of the Word for your life. *"The Word of God is the fulcrum upon which the lever of prayer is placed and by which things are mightily moved"* (Bounds, 66).

What does this praying the Word do? It greatly builds FAITH because *". . .faith cometh by hearing and hearing by the Word of God" (Romans 10:17)*. Further, Satan and all his demons tremble when you pray the Word of God. He knows you are not just praying your own words, but the Words of the One who will cast him into the "lake of fire". If you plan to pray The Word of God, there are certain faith-building scriptures about God that you must memorize or know how to paraphrase accurately as well as know where they are found.

> **"God is not a man, that he should lie; neither the son of man, that he should repent: hath he said, and shall he not do it? Or hath he spoken, and shall he not make it good?" (Numbers 23:19).**

> **"Jesus Christ, the same, yesterday, today, and forever" (Hebrews 13:8).**

> **"Then, Peter opened his mouth, and said, Of a truth I perceive God is no respecter of persons" (Acts 10:34).**

> **"The Lord is not slack concerning his promise, as some men count slackness; but is longsuffering to usward, not willing that any should perish, but that all should come to repentance" (II Peter 3:9).**

"For the Son of man is come to seek and to save that which was lost" (Luke 19:10).

HOW TO PRAY THE WORD

Identify areas of concern. Find the scriptures that identify with your need, the Word is truth and power. The Word of God is the only thing that will not pass away. **Pray what the Word says about your problem. Things will change.**

Children and Grandchildren

> *"Lo, Children are a heritage of the Lord; and the fruit of the womb is his reward (Psalms 127:3).*

> *"Behold, I and the children whom the Lord hath given me are for signs and wonders in Israel from the Lord of hosts, which dwelleth in mount Zion (Isaiah 8:18).*

> *"Fear not: for I am with thee: I will bring up thy seed from the east, and gather thee from the west; I will say to the north, Give up; and to the south, Keep not back: bring my sons from far, and my daughters from the ends of the earth" (Isaiah 43:5-6).*

> *"Children's children are the crown of old men; and the glory of children are their fathers" (Proverbs 17:6).*

Example of agreeing with God in prayer

"God, according to you Word, you said children are an inheritance from you and I thank you for them. Satan is trying and will try to destroy them but your Word said you would bring them back and use them in signs and wonders. God, I thank you, and I agree with your will for my children to be saved, blessed, and anointed. I will not fear because you came and died to save my children."

Children of Fatherless Homes

Children have the ear and heart of The Lord. He told His disciples to leave the children alone and let them come to Him. In some of our communities, 70% of all children are born to and/or grow up with single parents. This was as common in Bible days as it is now (Isaiah 54:1). Our task is to let all fatherless children know that God will work for them and support them if they serve Him.

> *"I delivered the poor that cried, and the fatherless, and him that had none to help him" (Job 29:12).*

> *". . .Thou art the helper of the fatherless, . . .thou wilt cause thine ear to hear; to judge the fatherless and the oppressed, that the man of the earth may man no more oppress" (Psalms 10:14, 17-18).*

> *"Ye shall not afflict any widow, or fatherless child. If thou afflict them in any wise, **and they cry at all unto me, I will surely hear their cry**. . ." (Exodus 22:22-23).*

*"A father of the fatherless, and a judge of the wid-
ows, is God in his holy habitation" (Psalms 68:5).*

*". . .In thee, the fatherless findeth mercy" (Hosea
14:3).*

Teach these children to pray, "Lord, I thank you because you
know how I feel and what I long for. I appreciate you being
my Father because You have everything that I need".

Children in Foster Care

Satan is doing some ugly things in families in this country.
We have too many children everywhere either in foster care
or "at risk" to foster care. It is the job of God's people to help
them survive the family's dysfunction.

*"When my father and my mother forsake me, then the
Lord will take me up" (Psalms 27:10).*

Teach them to pray, "God, I thank you because you know my
hurts, and I know you will take care of me. You are everywhere and have all power". Since God came to seek and to
save everybody, teach them to pray for their parents EVERY
DAY.

Prayers for Young People

*"Children obey your parents in the Lord: for this
is right. Honor thy father and mother; which is the
first commandment with promise; That it may be well*

with thee, and thou mayest live long on the earth"
(Ephesians 6:1-3).

"Children obey your parents in all things, for this is
well pleasing unto the Lord" (Colossians 3:20).

"Wherewithal shall a young man cleanse his way?
By taking heed thereunto according to thy Word"
(Psalms 119:9).

"Remember now thy Creator in the days of thy
youth, while the evil days come not, nor the years
draw nigh, when thou shalt say, I have no pleasure in
them" (Ecclesiastes 12:1).

"Be not over much wicked, neither be thou fool-
ish; why shouldest thou die before thy time?"
(Ecclesiastes 7:17).

We must teach our children and young people how to agree
with God in prayer for all the blessings He has stored up for
them.

"Lord Jesus, I thank You for my life and I choose to be
blessed. I will honor my parents according to Ephesians
6:1-3 and place my life into Your Hands now so evil and
destruction will not come near me."

Unsaved Relatives

"The Lord is not slack concerning his promise, as

some count slackness; but is longsuffering to usward, not willing that any should perish, but all should come to repentance" (II Peter 3:9).

"Who hath delivered us from the power of darkness, and hath translated us into the kingdom of his dear Son" (Colossians 1:13).

For example, personalize the prayers for your unsaved relatives: "Lord, I thank you because you came to seek and to save _____ and according to II Peter 3:9, you don't want (him, her, them) to perish. So according to your Word in Colossians 1:13, deliver _____ from the power of darkness and translate him (her,them) into your Kingdom. I thank you because I believe your Word and agree with your Word".

Revival in Your Church

"But in the last days it shall come to pass, that the mountain of the house of the Lord shall be established in the top of the mountains, and it shall be exalted above the hills; and people shall flow into it" (Micah 4:1).

"Wilt thou not revive us again; that thy people may rejoice in thee? Shew us thy mercy, O Lord, and grant us thy salvation" (Psalms 85:6-7; See Revelations 3:15-16).

"And it shall come to pass in the last days, saith God,

I will pour out of my Spirit upon all flesh: and your sons and daughters shall prophesy and your young men shall see visions, and your old men shall dream dreams: and on my servants and on my handmaidens I will pour out in those days of my Spirit; and they shall prophesy" (Acts 2:17-18).

"Call unto me, and I will answer thee, and show thee great and mighty things, which thou knowest not" (Jeremiah 33:3).

"Again I say unto you, that if two of you shall agree on earth as touching anything that they shall ask, it shall be done for them of my father which is heaven" (Matthew 18:19).

You don't have to have a lot of people to pray for revival. Get one or two persons that hunger for revival and pray: "Lord, we need revival, we want revival, we call on you according to Jeremiah 33:3 and we are looking for a mighty revival. These are the last days; pour out your Spirit as promised in Acts 2:17-18. We thank you God because your Word is true and we agree with your Word.

Healing

"Bless the Lord. . .Who forgiveth all thine iniquities; who healeth all thy diseases" (Psalm 103:2).

"But He was wounded for our transgressions, he was bruised for our iniquities: the chastisement of our

peace was upon Him; and with His stripes we are healed" (Isaiah 53:5).

". . .And He cast out spirits with His word and healed all that were sick: That it might be fulfilled which was spoken by Esaias the prophet, saying, Himself took our infirmities and bare our sicknesses" (Matthew 8:16-17).

"Who his own self bare our sins in his own body on the tree, that we, being dead to sins should live unto righteousness: by whose stripes ye were healed" (I Peter 2:24).

It is but a small thing for God to heal any and every thing because He is the God of all flesh. "God, thank you because I am healed right now. Your Word tells me in Isaiah 53:5 that I am healed and I Peter 2:24 says that I was healed. Your Word is eternal and powerful. I agree with your Word and I thank you for healing me".

There are many illnesses that afflict the saints and God does deliver them out of them all (Psalms 34:19). However find some illnesses and/or disease in the Bible which the Lord healed. Pray the Word, "Lord, you are the same yesterday, today, and forever and you change not. Just a couple of days ago, you healed the blind man. Heal my eyes. You made my eyes, you know about them. I thank you for your love, power, and changelessness" (The blind man in Mark 8:23). Incurable diseases whether cancer, multiple sclerosis, AIDS, or whatever, use the example of leprosy in Luke 17:11-19.

- For female problems of any kind, use the example of the woman with the issue of blood in Matthew 9:20.
- Arthritis and orthopedic problems use the paralyzed man in Matthew 9:2; or the impotent man in John 5:7; or the withered hand man in Matthew 12:10.

Personal Deliverance

"For the eyes of the Lord run to and fro throughout the whole earth, to show Himself strong in the behalf of them whose heart is perfect toward Him. . ." (II Chronicles 16:9).

"There hath no temptation taken you such as is common to man: but God is faithful, who will not suffer you to be tempted above that ye are able; but will with the temptation also make a way of escape, that ye may be able to bear it" (II Corinthians 10:13).

"And it shall come to pass, that whosoever shall call on the name of the Lord shall be delivered. . ." (Joel 2:32).

"He shall deliver thee in six troubles, yea in seven there shall no evil touch thee. In famine He shall redeem thee from death; and in war from the power of the sword. Thou shall be hid from the scourge of the tongue; neither shalt thou be afraid of destruction when it cometh" (Job 5:19-21).

Pray and agree with God. "I thank you that you are in control and you will not bring more on me than I can bear, so according to I Peter 5:7, I cast every care to you and I know according to Job 5:19, I am delivered out of these troubles."

"It cannot be stated too frequently that the life of a Christian includes much warfare, with intense conflict – a lifelong contest. It is a battle, moreover, waged against invisible foes, who are ever alert, and ever seeking to entrap, deceive, and ruin the souls of men. The life to which Holy Scripture calls men is no picnic. It entails effort, wrestling, struggling; it demands the putting forth of the full energy of the Spirit in order to frustrate the foe and to come off, at the last, more than a conqueror." (Bounds, 61)

Financial Miracles

"Bring ye all the tithes into the storehouse, that there may be meat in mine house, and prove me now herewith, saith the Lord of hosts, if I will not open you the windows of heaven, and pour you out a blessing, that there shall not be room enough to receive it. And I will rebuke the devourer for your sakes. . ." (Malachi 3:10-11).

"And it shall come to pass, if thou shalt hearken diligently unto the voice of the Lord thy God to observe and to do all his commandments which I command thee this day. . .Blessed shall be thy basket and thy store" (Deuteronomy 28:1,5).

". . .And the wealth of the sinner is laid up for the

just" (Proverbs 13:22).

Pray: "Lord, I thank you that you are the same God that gave wealth to Abraham, Isaac, and Jacob and you store up the wealth of the wicked for the righteous. I am glad to obey and pay tithes and give offering. Now God, I thank you for releasing finances and wealth in my life."

Freedom from Fear

Matthew 10:30-31

> *"Fear thou not, for I am with thee; be not dismayed, for I am thy God: I will strengthen thee; yea, I will help thee; yea, I will uphold thee with the right hand of my righteousness" (Isaiah 41:10).*

> *". . .I have called thee by thy name: thou are mine. When thou passest through the waters, I will be with thee; and through the rivers, they shall not overflow thee; when thou walkest through the fire, thou shalt not be burned; neither shall the flame kindle upon thee" (Isaiah 43:1-2).*

> *". . .For he hath said, I will never leave thee, nor forsake thee. So that we may boldly say, The Lord is my helper, and I will not fear what man shall do unto me" (Hebrews 13:5-6).*

> *"I will not be afraid of ten thousands of people, that have set themselves against me round about"*

(Psalms 3:6).

"The Lord is on my side; I will not fear; What can man do unto me?" (Psalms 118:6).

Freedom from Torment

"Thou will keep him in perfect peace whose mind is stayed on thee because he trusteth in thee" (Isaiah 26:3).

"Peace I leave with you, my peace I give unto you; not as the world giveth, give I unto you. Let not your heart be troubled, neither let it be afraid" (John 14:27).

"Be careful for nothing; but in everything by prayer and supplication with thanksgiving let your requests be made known unto God. And the peace of God, which passeth all understanding, shall keep your hearts and minds through Christ Jesus" (Philippians 4:6-7).

"For God hath not given us the spirit of fear; but of power, and of love, and of a sound mind" (II Timothy 1:7).

"Lord, I thank you because You are my peace giver. I will stay in Your Word and praise You because I trust You. I do not have to fret or worry because You are the God of everything and I am yours. I thank You for the peace and love that

You have given me."

Healing from Loneliness and Rejection

> *"For I will restore health unto thee, and I will heal thee of thy wounds, saith the Lord; because they called thee an Outcast saying, this is Zion whom no man seeketh after" (Jeremiah 30:17).*

> *"Let your conversation be without covetousness; and be content with such things as ye have: for he hath said, I will never leave thee nor forsake thee" (Hebrews 13:5).*

"Lord thank You because You will never leave me alone or comfortless. You understand how I feel because on the cross everyone left You and forsook You, and I gladly open to your fellowship and healing right now. I thank You I am not alone or rejected because I belong to the King of kings and Lord of lords."

Freedom from Depression

> *"To appoint unto them that mourn in Zion, to give unto them beauty for ashes, the oil of joy for mourning, **the garment of praise for the spirit of heaviness;** that they might be called the trees of righteousness, the planting of the Lord, that he might be glorified" (Isaiah 61:3).*

"Lord I am tired of being depressed, feeling depressed, and

looking depressed. Thank You because according to Isaiah 61:3, You have given me the garment of praise. I choose to dress, wrap myself up in, and wear the garment of praise. Lord, I glorify, worship, and honor You because You are worthy."

Remember God enters the praises of his people (Psalms 22:3) and the devil can't stay where God is. Depression must go!

Freedom from Contamination from Sexual Filth including Incest and Rape

"But if ye do not forgive, neither will your Father which is in heaven forgive your trespasses" (Mark 11:26).

"Looking diligently lest any man fail the grace of God; lest any root of bitterness springing up trouble you, and thereby many be defiled" (Hebrews 12:15).

It is hard and difficult to let the pain and filth go when you have been violated. The abuser left a residue of filth, low self-esteem, and unworthiness. God is not able to cleanse all of that stuff out when the victim harbors unforgiveness, bitterness, and maybe hatred. **These are more of Satan's deposits in your life; the ripple effect from the abuse.** Pray, "Lord, I will not allow Satan to manipulate me through his demons of unforgiveness and keep me out of fellowship with You. I agree and obey your Word; I forgive all that have messed over me in my life. I let it go and make room for your cleansing -- healing my mind, my dreams, my desires, and my emotions. I thank You for forgiving me for my unforgiveness."

Pray the Word and Get Results

Write out your prayer request list and date it. Next to each prayer request, write appropriate scripture(s). Every few months, do a new list because you will find God is answering according to His Word. There is no special time to pray about needs and concerns. According to Luke 18:1, men ought always pray and not faint (not give up) anyhow. Some scriptures that are important, you may not remember. Write them on three by five index cards. Carry them with you all the time. PRAY THE WORD about your need, when you are stuck in traffic. During your week night prayer services, PRAY THE WORD about your need. Instead of watching television, PRAY THE WORD about your need, while laying in bed at night.

God cannot lie and His Word does not lie. When praying the Word, you are agreeing with Truth. EXPECT VICTORY!!

"But thanks be to God, which giveth us the victory through our Lord Jesus Christ. Therefore, be ye steadfast, unmoveable, always abounding in the work of the Lord, forasmuch as ye know that your labor is not in vain the Lord" (1 Corinthians 15:57,58).

LEARN TO PRAY
WARFARE PRAYERS

In these times, every person who is born again does not have a choice. Satan has but a few days. Get it in your spirit that you are invincible in the presence of Satan and his demons because Jesus made us "kings and priests unto God by washing us in His Own Blood" (Revelations 1:5-6). And Satan is just prince and only over those who are not washed in the Blood of Jesus. Don't hesitate to pray those scriptures which assure your invincibility.

> *"Verily, I say unto you, whatsoever ye shall bind on earth shall be bound in heaven: and whatsoever ye shall loose on earth shall be loosed in heaven"* *(Matthew 18:18).*

> *"For we wrestle not against flesh and blood, but against principalities, against powers, against the rulers of the darkness of this world, against spiritual wickedness in high places" (Ephesians 6:12).*

> *"For the weapons of our warfare are not carnal, but mighty through God to the pulling down of*

strongholds. . ." (II Corinthians 10:4).

"Ye are of God, little children, and have overcome them: because greater is he that is in you than he that is in the world" (I John 4:4).

"And they overcame him by the Blood of the Lamb, and by the word of their testimony; and they loved not their lives unto the death" (Revelations 12:11).

"And he said unto them, I beheld Satan as lightning fall from heaven. Behold, I give unto you power to tread on serpents and scorpions, and over all the power of the enemy: and nothing shall by any means hurt you" (Luke 10:18-19).

Tell the devil, boldly, and in absolute confidence. ***"I have power over all your power according to Luke 10:19. I take authority over you and all the plans you are orchestrating against my life, my family, my church, and my community. I agree with the POWER OF GOD. I choose not to fail and I won't fail. In the NAME OF JESUS OF NAZARETH, I bind, rebuke, renounce, and cast you out. Right now, I render you ineffective and powerless by the shed blood of the Lamb of God."*** Pray these prayers and mean it.

In Deliverance

When an individual is severely oppressed of the devil or possessed by the devil, you must use the scriptures to discomfit the enemy and weaken his hold and make him want to leave.[7] Satan hates the truth especially when it applies to him. Just quote these

(and other) scriptures as many times as necessary to make the devil vacate.

> *"Wherefore God also hath highly exalted him, and given him a name which is above every name: That at the Name of Jesus EVERY knee shall bow, of things in heaven, and things in the earth, and things under the earth; And that every tongue should confess that Jesus Christ is Lord, to the glory of God the Father"* *(Philippians 2:9-11).*

Satan knows the Word and knows that he is going to have to confess that Jesus is Lord, but he HATES to hear it. Quote the scripture as often as necessary during a deliverance session.

> *"And the devil that deceived them was cast into the lake of fire and brimstone, where the beast and the false prophet are, and shall be tormented day and night for ever and ever"* *(Revelations 20:10).*

> *"And having spoiled all principalities and powers, He made a show of them openly, triumphing over them in it"* *(Colossians 2:15).*

Remember you are not only an overcomer but a warrior against all those things that Satan sends against you to "steal,

---

7   There are many other strategies used in deliverance like repentance, binding and rebuking, singing songs about the Blood of Jesus, etc. Here we are just addressing the use of the Word of God in deliverance.

kill, and destroy". Therefore it is your job to dominate the environment; you rule in this spiritual kingdom. That's why you pray "thy kingdom come, thy will be done in earth as it is in heaven". Pray aggressively, plead the Blood of Jesus, quote scriptures. The battle belongs to the Lord and it has already been won.

"THE ONE CONCERN OF THE DEVIL IS TO KEEP CHRISTIANS FROM PRAYING. HE FEARS NOTHING FROM PRAYERLESS STUDIES, PRAYERLESS WORK, AND PRAYERLESS RELIGION. HE LAUGHS AT OUR TOIL, MOCKS AT OUR WISDOM, BUT TREMBLES WHEN WE PRAY" Samuel Chadwick *(1832 -1917).*

CONCLUSION

Prayer is the one absolute essential for success in God; it is not an optional or recommended choice. All prayer, -- private, concert church prayer, and continuous prayer are mandated by God.

The world, moving at a horrible pace, is manipulated by Satan. It is said, for example, that 50% of all new web sites are pornographic. The only difference is made by those who take time to pray. We must come another way and pray at the faith level of God's awesome might.

- **Pray the Word of God and pray** for revival.
- **Pray the Word of God and pray** against the ancient Canaanite demons of Baal, which included child prostitution, male and female prostitution, adultery, fornication, rape, pedophilia, and incest.
- **Pray the Word in power and pray** against the ancient demons of Babylon – pride, greed, hunger for wealth, arrogance.
- **Pray the Word of God and pray** against the subtle but powerful operations of the ancient demons of Leviathan, pride, insanity and psychosis, demons of delusion and deception, and demons blocking the

Word (even with sleeping and drowsiness).
- **Pray the Word and pray** against the abominable, witchcraft, and rebellion. Not only is the occult proliferating but some of your doctors, co-workers, and even the teachers of your children are Satanists.

Satan is trying to roll over the church community like a bull dozer or shock troops. Our weapon of powerful aggression and satanic destruction is prayer and fasting. When the body of Christ and individuals pray, then,

> *"No weapon that is formed against thee shall prosper; and every tongue that shall rise against thee in judgment thou shalt condemn. This is the heritage of the servants of the Lord, and their righteousness is of me, saith the Lord" (Isaiah 54:17).*

Yes, this is the time of the "falling away" (II Thessalonians 2:3), BUT GOD HAS NOT CHANGED. *Yes, this is the time of the forms of godliness without power* (II Timothy 3:5), BUT GOD HAS NOT CHANGED. *It seems like history is repeating itself but there is nothing new under the sun* (Ecclesiates 1:9-10); remember GOD HAS NOT CHANGED.

> *"There is a conspiracy of her prophets, . . .her priests have violated my law. . . , her princes in the midst thereof are like ravening wolves, . . .to get dishonest gain; the prophets. . .divining lies, saying thus saith the Lord when the Lord hath not spoken" (Ezekiel 22:25-28).*

Even though we may experience some of what Ezekiel cried out against, God still responds to the prayer warrior. God is still seeking for the man, woman, boy, or girl to stand in the gap (Ezekiel 22:30).

*"**If my people**, which are called by my name **shall humble themselves**, and **pray**, and seek my face, and turn from their wicked ways; then will I hear from heaven and forgive their sin and heal their land" (2 Chronicles 7:14-15).*

God is ready for His remnant to work in His end-time revival. It will come but only as a result of much prayer. However, God cannot even speak to you and use you as an instrument when you are filling your leisure time by attending Satan's church – watching many of the shows on television.

Pray earnestly and continuously. If you give yourself two hours of leisure time activities, give God two hours of prayer and studying the Word. You are not greater than God, so give God more time than you give yourself. Bishop Charles Harrison Mason, the founder of the Church of God in Christ, prayed six hours or more on his knees every day and would call on the Name of Jesus sometimes for two hours without stopping. My father, an early member of his South Wellington Street church said that he was the only man he knew that had worn his shoes out in the toes from the many hours on his knees.

Prayer is the mainspring of the spiritual life of a church. LORD GIVE US SOME PRAYING MEN! Cultivate a life of prayer and watch God work. We really do not have a choice. *"PRAY WITHOUT CEASING" (I Thessalonians 5:17).*

> *"And now brethren, I commend you to God and to the word of his grace, which is able to build you up and give you an inheritance among all them that are sanctified" (Acts 20:32).*

BIBLIOGRAPHY

The Holy Bible. King James Version (KJV)

The Holy Bible. New International Version (NIV)

E.M. Bounds. Complete Work on Prayer

Fay Ellis Butler. Called To Be Saints

Draper, Edythe. Draper's Book of Quotations from the Christian

World, (Tyndale House Publications, Wheaton, Illinois).

Marilyn Hickey. The Names of God

Andrew Murray. The Ministry of Intercession

OTHER BOOKS BY THE AUTHOR

After Deliverance, Then What? ($5.00)

Called To Be Saints ($12.00)

Called To Be Warriors ($15.00)

Sex: Abuse, Pain, Deliverance ($15.00)

How To Minister To Christians in Bondage ($5.00).

The Holy Ghost: Don't Live Here and Leave Here Without Him ($12.00).

The Destruction Of Our Children Why They Must Become Warriors ($7.00).

Rejection, the Ruling Spirit ($15.00)

The Ignorance Crisis ($12.00).

Why Are God's People Sick? ($5.00).

Order from Amazon.com or from

Dr. Fay Ellis Butler
P.0. Box 330995
Stuyvesant Station
Brooklyn, New York, 11233

ABOUT THE AUTHOR

FAY ELLIS BUTLER was raised in the Church of God in Christ, the daughter of a pastor, Rev. Ralph N. Ellis, Sr. After completing her secondary education in the public schools of New York City, she attended Bellevue/New York University School of Nursing and graduated as a Registered Nurse. Later, she matriculated at Queens College of the City University of New York and graduated *cum laude* in 1971 with her Bachelor's degree. She was accepted as a doctoral fellow at Columbia University and was a National Institute of Mental Health Trainee receiving her Master's degree in 1974, her second Master's in 1975, and finally graduating from Columbia University with a Ph.D. in Medical Anthropology in 1982.

Fay uses her talents, skills, and energies working with and for people in secular and church settings. Among her many activities, although not limited to these, are the seminars and workshops she conducts on marriage, singles, parenting, and intergenerational conflicts (adolescent problems). She is a successful proposal writer totaling over $5,000,000 in grants. She works as a Health and Nutrition Consultant. In the church, she is a Sunday school teacher, Bible school teacher, prayer leader, and evangelist.

She was married to the late John Louis Butler, an attorney and pastor in Brooklyn, New York and she is blessed with seven children, eight grandchildren, and 1 great grandson.

CPSIA information can be obtained
at www.ICGtesting.com
Printed in the USA
LVHW022350250219
608763LV00003B/91